Contents

A desert habitat

A desert is an area of land.
A desert is hot and dry.

A desert has living things.
A desert has non-living things.

Lizard

black collared lizard

Is a lizard a living thing?

Does a lizard need food? *Yes.*
Does a lizard need water? *Yes.*

Does a lizard need air? *Yes.*

Does a lizard grow? *Yes.*

So a lizard is a living thing.

Cactus

Is a cactus a living thing?

Sunshine makes plant food.

Does a cactus need food? *Yes.*
Does a cactus need water? *Yes.*

Does a cactus need air? *Yes.*

Does a cactus grow? *Yes.*

So a cactus is a living thing.

Rock

Is a rock a living thing?

Does a rock need food? *No.*
Does a rock need water? *No.*

Does a rock need air? *No.*

Does a rock grow? *No.*

So a rock is not a living thing.

Scorpion

Is a scorpion a living thing?

centipede

Does a scorpion need food? *Yes.*
Does a scorpion need water? *Yes.*

19

Does a scorpion need air? *Yes.*

Does a scorpion grow? *Yes.*

So a scorpion is a living thing.

A desert is home to many things.

A desert is an important habitat.

Picture glossary

 **cactus** a plant that grows in the desert

 **desert** a habitat that is hot and dry in the day. Deserts can be cold at night.

 **habitat** area where plants and animals live

Index

Notes for Parents and Teachers
Before reading
Talk about what living things need – food, water, and air. Talk about things that move but which are not living – cars, boats, planes. How do they move?
After reading
Give one child a picture such as a boat, tree, or baby. The child must not show the picture to the rest of the class. Encourage the other children to ask questions to guess what the picture shows. First they must determine if the thing is living or non-living (needs food, water, and air, and it grows). Then they can ask other questions: Does it move? Does it travel on land? Is there one in the classroom?
Talk about how babies grow, from lying on its back to rolling on to its tummy, siting up, crawling, toddling, walking, andrunning. Ask the children to do each of the actions of the "growing" story.